FINANCIAL FEMINIST

Master Your Money and Create the Life You Love Despite the Patriarchy's Cr*p

Daisy Hill

Disclaimer

ISBN: 9798882932700

Daisy Hill

Daisy Hill

Introduction

Welcome to the revolution in personal finance! In a world where the financial deck has been stacked against women for far too long, it's time to take control of your money and your life. I'm thrilled to introduce you to "Financial Feminist: Master Your Money and Create the Life You Love Despite the Patriarchy's Crap," your ultimate guide to reclaiming your financial power and building the life of your dreams.

"Financial Feminist: Master Your Money and Create the Life You Love Despite the Patriarchy's Cr*p," the definitive manual for taking back control of your finances and creating the life you've always wanted. creating a solid financial foundation and making space in the financial world will allow you to live the life you desire both now and in retirement. Get ready to unleash your financial strength and pave your path toward a time when equality is vital.

Daisy Hill

In what way does this book benefit women readers? Allow me to explain.

It's time to break through the rich glass ceiling first and foremost. Women still earn less than males on average despite making up half of the workforce, and they have difficulties when it comes to accumulating money and reaching financial independence. But have no fear— "Financial Feminist" is here to provide you with the information, resources, and perspective you need to get past these challenges and succeed financially.

Second, empowerment is at the heart of financial feminism rather than merely money. It's about identifying and combating the institutionalized biases and inequality that prevent women from advancing in the field of personal finance. The pink tax, the gender pay gap, and the underrepresentation of women in financial institutions are only a few examples of the patriarchal dynamics that "Financial Feminist" reveals and provides tools to combat.

Most significant, though, is that you ought to lead a prosperous, free, and contented life.

Daisy Hill

"Financial Feminist" means using money as a tool to design the life you want, not just accumulating wealth for its own sake. Whether you want to buy a house, travel the world, launch your own company, or live comfortably in retirement, this book will show you ways to bring it about according to your schedule.

Within these pages, you will learn:

- ✓ Techniques for negotiating the pay you deserve and bridging the gender pay gap.

- ✓ Advice on investing, saving, and budgeting based on your financial situation and objectives.

- ✓ Insights into the psychology of money and the development of an empowered and abundant mindset.

- ✓ Advice on managing the many aspects of personal finance, such as debt, insurance, and retirement planning, as well as taxes.

- ✓ Tales and lessons from trailblazing women who have succeeded financially on their terms, despite all the obstacles.

Daisy Hill

Are you prepared to become a member of the financial feminist movement? Are you prepared to take charge of your life and finances? If this is the case, read "Financial Feminist" and together we can rewrite the laws of wealth. When Women who are financially empowered can negotiate for a salary and use strategies to close the gender wage gap, which benefits all of us.

A financial feminist is a woman who uses the power of money to better herself and those around her. She is on a mission to dismantle the status quo by offering practical solutions and a route to success and financial independence, as well as to educate women about personal finance and the structural oppression that makes it particularly difficult for them to accumulate wealth.

The Goal
The intention is for women to achieve financial independence so that they can use their earnings to pursue their interests. Would you like to become a parent? Would you rather spend five years traveling the world? You are free to choose these things without relying on the money of others if you have financial independence.

Daisy Hill

James Brown released "It's a Man's World," a song that captured the essence of the time, in the middle of the 1960s. A million copies of the song were sold. (Who bought it, I wonder?) James Brown was singing of a global mindset that permeates all nations and civilizations. In essence, such a mindset says, "This world was meant for men, even though women are here."

It's made with men in mind. Women only step in when they are needed. It's a man's world; you women keep to yourself." Is man the owner of the world? What role do women play in it, if any?

Financial feminism dispels financial fallacies and highlights the structural oppression that traps many people in unsatisfactory employment or debt cycles presenting doable strategies that anyone can implement right now to reduce the pay gap, improve financial stability, and create the life they have always wanted.

Overview

A financial feminist is a woman who makes use of the influence of money to better herself and those around her. Her mission is to provide women with the knowledge and skills necessary to manage their finances

Daisy Hill

and achieve financial stability, including budgeting, saving, spending, negotiating salary, and investing.

They can then accept the battle against the current financial system that deprives so many women of their rights by doing this.

Who Should Read Financial Feminist?

- ✓ Anyone feeling stuck living paycheck to paycheck.

- ✓ Those who want to retire someday.

- ✓ Anyone frustrated by the sexist wealth gap looking to build a more equal future.

Daisy Hill

CHAPTER ONE
The Emotion of Money:
"Dismantling the Barriers of Financial Preconceptions"

Our financial decisions are often driven by our emotions, which have an impact on all from our spending and saving habits to our perceptions of success and riches. In "Financial Feminist: Master Your Money and Create the Life You Love Despite the Patriarchy's Cr*p," we examine how emotions and money are intricately related, particularly when viewed from a gender angle.

Money is a complicated network of feelings, ideas, and cultural norms that influence our relationship with it. It is far greater than physical money. From childhood, we develop attitudes and preconceptions about money that influence every financial decision we make. These misconceptions frequently serve as obstacles that keep us from reaching financial independence and contentment.

Daisy Hill

Money is much more than just a tool for trade; it has a profound impact on our feelings, convictions, and moral principles. Our views and behaviors about money are shaped by the messages we are exposed to about it from an early age, which come from our families, communities, and the media. This chapter will examine the nuanced emotional terrain surrounding money and how it affects our financial choices.

Get ready to break free from the constraints that patriarchy places on your financial life, reclaim financial mastery, and forge a new path that leads to both financial fulfillment and liberation from financial slavery. It's time to create a gender-neutral future for financial empowerment and rethink the emotional terrain of money.

You can't begin to alter your financial tales until you are truthful about their origins. Someone cannot be taught how to establish budgetary targets if they are unaware of the consequences of their financial hang-ups. We explore in detail the emotional landscape around money in this chapter. The constant social pressures placed on women to adhere to certain views and actions around money

Daisy Hill

resulted in the entrainment of stereotypes and prejudices in our connection with it.

To fight these stereotypes, we here debunk the idea that women are inherently less knowledgeable or skilled in financial concerns. Instead, we investigate the powerful emotions that are connected to our financial decisions, such as ambition, fear, guilt, and passion, and how they shape our financial narratives.

The Psychology Behind Money

Money has psychological effects. Our mindsets and emotions at any given time have a direct influence on our financial decisions, which in turn influence our long-term results. Our feelings about money are frequently a result of our early life experiences and the lessons we were taught as children.

Money can evoke feelings of shortage or worry in some people, nevertheless, it can also be linked to security and abundance in others. We can simplify the complexity of our relationship with money if we comprehend the causes of these feelings.

Daisy Hill

Primarily, we must acknowledge that financial stability is heavily influenced by psychology. Our thoughts and emotions at any given time have a direct influence on the financial decisions we make. Our longer-term results are strongly impacted by these financial choices. We need to examine our emotions to make long-lasting financial changes.

We have both positive and negative feelings regarding every facet of money, including income, debt, and investment. Our everyday relationship with money is determined by our thoughts, feelings, and mindset. It extends beyond daily expenses and budgetary planning; larger financial decisions are also influenced by our emotions, even in the way we see money and the individuals who possess it.

Our purchasing patterns and investing choices can be influenced by ideas like loss aversion, status-seeking, and FOMO. We can become more conscious of these psychological influences on our financial conduct by comprehending these psychological drivers. Nobody is impervious.

Daisy Hill

Unique Financial Challenges Women Face

Shame is the most prevalent of these financial emotions. Shame is a common, fear-based, social feeling that we all encounter daily. Shame makes us feel undeserving and unacceptably human and is a result of our dread of being abandoned.

It has a strong association with eating disorders, depression, addiction, hostility, and violence. Women encounter difficulties in securing a prosperous financial future.

The Impacts of Culture and Society on our money thoughts are significantly shaped by cultural and societal standards. Certain cultures may view riches as a sign of achievement and social standing, whereas other cultures may view wealth negatively or value modesty more. These factors have the power to significantly alter our financial decisions and how we see ourselves concerning money.

Shame

How often have you heard that discussing money is impolite? Or inquire about the salaries of your colleagues? Women are indoctrinated from an early age to avoid addressing money matters.

Daisy Hill

Daisy Hill

They are taught that it is impolite to even inquire about finances. It is a deeply embedded idea with a sexist foundation. It should come as no surprise that women develop shame-based attitudes toward money and finances that persist into adulthood. But how can women succeed if they never discuss money?

How can they develop and learn? It has only recently been that ideas like pay transparency and candid conversations about issues like retirement, literacy, and income gaps have gained traction.

The greatest approach to get over this embarrassment in the interim is to change your viewpoint. "When you are clear on your values and you know your worth, and what you bring to the world, it is easy to talk about money. Because money is just an expression of your values," Kim Constable, CEO of The Sculpted Vegan, told Forbes.

Money or the way you use it can certainly be an expression of your values. For example, do you put your hard-earned paycheck into a retirement account because you value safety and security? Do you buy clothes to make yourself feel better emotionally?

Daisy Hill

Consider taking some time to reflect on how you use your money and whether it aligns with your ideal values.

Lack of understanding

How many times have you started a conversation with someone about the stock market (or, rather, get dragged into a conversation by someone who thinks they know all about stocks) only to feel like you don't understand what the other person is saying?

The stock market comes with its own set of jargon and vocabulary, and most people are not taught what words like "short" and "mutual fund" mean. Wealth managers with bad intentions will often hide behind jargon to make themselves feel more important by making you feel like investing is something you'll never understand.

The first step to becoming more comfortable with the world of investing and finances? Understanding that although it may seem scary or intimidating, it's a lot more straightforward than a lot of us originally thought.

"Anyone can learn about adding a mix of stocks and bonds," Stacy Francis, president, and CEO of wealth management firm Francis Financial, told CNBC.

Daisy Hill

"It's not about choosing a hot stock or the best investment. It is a lot more boring than people believe. You choose an ideal asset allocation and stick with it." The truth is that women have all the behavioral traits to become great investors to set up their financial future. It's okay not to know everything about the stock market — sometimes, you just need to get started and figure it out slowly or enlist the help of an advisor you trust.

Lack of guidance

Women don't receive the same financial advice and financial guidance as men, making it more difficult for women to achieve financial success later in life. Most women growing up don't receive enough education or encouragement about finances. That means they may be offered more expensive financial products when they do see a financial advisor. It can also mean receiving less education about financial investing and budgeting.

"Financial education can be daunting. There are a million ways to earn a million dollars, but where does one start as a woman in business? Can financial advisors be trusted, or are they quota and commission-driven?

Daisy Hill

We can take control of our financial future and the best place to start is by educating ourselves," it is those out-of-control feelings we experience whenever we're worried that something undesirable about us has been or is about to be exposed.

Many studies have found that shame is highly correlated with violence, aggression, bullying, depression, addiction, and eating disorders, because we're taught almost nothing about our negative emotions, except to be afraid of them, to shut them down. As a result, we confuse them with who we are.

To reframe shame from a crushing emotional burden to a simple message from your brain, start by reaching out and connecting with someone else. Partner up with others who want to learn what you want to learn, who are willing to admit what they don't know, and who will celebrate one another's differences.

We don't log in to our financial accounts because we're too scared of what we'll find. We feel ashamed for not understanding what a 401(k) is, so we don't ask. We feel guilty asking for a raise since maybe we "haven't earned it."
Daisy Hill

Daisy Hill

Facing the unknown, doing something that feels uncomfortable and new, and allowing ourselves to admit that we don't have all the answers is one of the bravest things we can do.

So, in the spirit of vulnerability, we're going to focus now on the emotional side of money good, bad, and ugly, and how we can use more of our money to bring us joy, comfort, and stability.

Financial and Emotional Triggers come to money, certain situations or occurrences can serve as emotional triggers. A financial setback, an unexpected economic windfall, or a significant life move like purchasing a home or beginning a family can all cause a range of feelings, from delight and enthusiasm to dread and worry. We can better control these triggers if we are aware of our emotional reactions to them.

This chapter offers guidance employing perceptive tales, empirically supported evaluation, and practical recommendations, motivating readers to accept their feelings and rework their financial plans.

Daisy Hill

We give ourselves how we can make deliberate, independent decisions.

Self-Esteem

The Function of Self-Esteem is the sense of self-worth that is frequently correlated with our financial success or failure, which can cause us to feel inadequate or ashamed when we don't meet our standards. It's critical to understand that neither our bank account balance nor our material belongings define who we are as people. To truly achieve financial freedom, one must develop a sense of self-worth that is unaffected by outside financial circumstances.

In "The Emotions of Money," we will explore the complexities of **how societal expectations, cultural norms, and individual experiences shape our emotional connection to finances.** From the fear of scarcity instilled in us to the guilt associated with spending time on ourselves, we unravel the layers of emotions that impact our financial behaviors.

Through empowering insights, real-life stories, and practical strategies, we aim to liberate readers from the emotional chains imposed by the patriarchal narrative Daisy Hill surrounding money. By acknowledging and understanding these emotions, we take the first step toward reclaiming our financial autonomy.

Understand Your Money Memory

Your money mindset is linked to the behaviors you saw your parents exhibit when managing their own money. One of the best ways to change your money mindset is to journal through a first money memory.

"Hear me roar, I am a woman." I don't know about you, but I'm not in the mood to fight or roar! I think I can be heard if I talk in a regular tone that I'm able to accomplish tasks while remaining motionless. Instead of inciting conflict, I can generate inspiration, so that from my house, I can influence a country, that my faith has the power to move mountains. It's time to solve this, not only for your happiness but also for the harmony of all that comes from your kingdom, your house, your place of employment, your church, your neighborhood, your city, your state, and your country. Your claim to all of eternity.

Daisy Hill

Now is the moment to talk.

- ✓ This exercise will help you understand your financial hang-ups and how you can start to fortify your financial foundation.

- ✓ It's time to act and change your relationship with money.

- ✓ Invest time and energy in educational resources.

- ✓ Open a savings account or IRA.

- ✓ Write down all debts.

- ✓ Rework your budget with a critical eye.

- ✓ Changing your mindset means overcoming negative beliefs about money that were learned at a young age. Money should not be seen as scarce or evil.

Unpacking your money memories, biases, and narratives can help you release shame and judgment. You will feel pride, awe, hope, and joy instead of shame, stress, and fear. Money opens every possibility for you, every comfort, every luxury.
Daisy Hill

The Five Financial Narratives

Financial narratives are common stories or mindsets that keep you   from becoming financially educated, stable, and confident. They are the hoops you must jump through to assemble your financial foundation.

1. **The Lottery Mentality**: Believing in windfall gains, such as winning the lottery, as a viable financial strategy can discourage people from saving and investing in a disciplined manner. It's essential to understand the value of consistent and informed financial planning.

2. **Debt as a Norm**: Assuming that debt is a natural and unavoidable part of life can lead to a cycle of perpetual indebtedness. While some debts may be necessary, understanding the difference between good and bad debt is crucial for financial well-being.

3. **The Illusion of Infinite Income**: Relying on the belief that one will always earn more money in the future can hinder effective budgeting and savings. Understanding the importance of living within one's means and saving Daisy Hill

for the future is crucial for long-term financial stability.

4. **Short-Term Investment Expectations**: Expecting quick and substantial returns on investments without considering the risks can lead to poor financial decisions. It's essential to have realistic expectations about investment returns and to focus on long-term financial goals.

5. **Ignoring Financial Education**: Dismissing the importance of financial education and assuming that financial matters are too complex can prevent individuals from taking control of their financial well-being. Developing financial literacy is key to making informed money decisions.

These narratives can influence individuals' financial behaviors and may hinder the development of financial literacy. Overcoming these misconceptions involves education, awareness, and a commitment to adopting sound financial practices.

Here is a roadmap to navigate and harness these emotions, transforming them from limitations into tools Daisy Hill for empowerment. It is about rewriting the narrative, embracing confidence in financial decision-making, and fostering a new relationship with money, one that is rooted in self-worth, resilience, and empowerment.

Join us on this transformative journey as we unpack the emotions of money, redefine financial freedom on our terms, and pave the way for a future where financial empowerment transcends gender stereotypes.

5 Thought-Provoking Questions

- ✓ What are some of your first financial memories or encounters?

- ✓ What effects do society or cultural standards have on your perceptions of success and wealth?

- ✓ What feelings do you connect money with, and how do those feelings affect the way you make money decisions?

- ✓ What are some typical sources of worry or tension in your life related to money?

- ✓ What impact does your self-worth have on your

Daisy Hill

relationship with money?

Daisy Hill

CHAPTER TWO
Spending

An essential component of our financial lives, spending frequently has social and emotional ramifications. After reading "Financial Feminist: Master Your Money and Create the Life You Love Despite the Patriarchy's Cr*p," we are better equipped to address the complexities of spending by looking at them from a male perspective. understanding and challenging the traditional gender norms and power dynamics that influence financial decision-making

Spending is not just transactional; **"Spending: Redefining Financial Liberation,"** challenges that idea. We look at how cultural norms impose financial restrictions on women, causing them to feel guilty or ashamed about pursuing their interests or themselves.

Here, we give readers the tools they need to change the way they feel about money. It's about realizing that our spending is an expression of our values, passions, a n d self-care, not just about making financial decisions.

Daisy Hill

By letting go of the guilt and taking back authority over our spending patterns, we open the door to financial independence.

Understand How You Spend Money

Everyone has a way of managing their finances. Many people learn how to manage their money by watching their parents or their friends. Our family story and experience play a significant role in how we learn to manage our finances.

Recognizing and Dispelling Financial Myths

One of the biggest challenges we confront on the path to financial freedom is the pervasiveness of deeply rooted financial stereotypes. These assumptions are frequently based on cultural narratives, gender standards, and societal norms that influence our views about money from a young age.

This chapter will examine the many financial stereotypes that disproportionately impact women and provide techniques for dispelling and overcoming them. Understanding how you spend money can be key to building a successful financial future, challenging the traditional gender norms and power dynamics that influence financial decision-making. For example, if you know you overspend on certain expenses, you can take steps to curb your habits or regulate them. Knowing your strengths and weaknesses can help you better manage your money. Being mindful is key. At the end of the month, make sure to track your progress and understand how you can improve. Here's an exploration:

1. **Conscious Consumption**: Financial feminism encourages individuals to practice conscious consumption, which involves being mindful of where and how money is spent. This means considering the ethical and social implications of purchasing decisions, supporting businesses that align with feminist values, and avoiding companies that perpetuate harmful gender stereotypes.

2. **Investing in Yourself**: Financial feminism prioritizes investing in oneself, both personally and professionally. This can include allocating funds for education, skill development, self-care, and career advancement. By investing in yourself, you empower yourself to break

through the barriers imposed by the patriarchal system and pursue your goals and aspirations.

3. **Closing the Wage Gap**: One of the central tenets of financial feminism is advocating for equal pay and closing the gender wage gap. This involves challenging workplace discrimination, negotiating for fair compensation, and supporting policies and initiatives that promote gender equality in the workforce. By earning what you're worth, you can build greater financial security and independence.

4. **Supporting Women-Owned Businesses**: Financial feminism emphasizes supporting women-owned businesses and initiatives to promote economic empowerment and gender equity. This can involve consciously directing spending towards businesses owned and operated by women, as well as advocating for policies that support female entrepreneurship and leadership.

5. **Investing with Purpose**: Financial feminism encourages investing with purpose, aligning investment decisions with values such as gender equality, environmental sustainability, and social justice. This may involve investing in companies with diverse leadership teams, supporting funds that prioritize gender-lens Daisy Hill

investing, or divesting from industries that perpetuate gender inequality.

6. **Building Financial Literacy**: Financial feminism recognizes the importance of financial literacy, particularly for women who have historically been marginalized in financial decision-making. This involves educating oneself about personal finance topics such as budgeting, saving, investing, and retirement planning, empowering women to take control of their financial futures.

7. **Challenging Patriarchal Narratives**: Finally, financial feminism involves challenging patriarchal narratives and norms that perpetuate inequality and limit women's financial autonomy. This may include questioning societal expectations around gender roles, advocating for policies that support work-life balance and caregiving responsibilities, and rejecting the notion that women are inherently less capable or knowledgeable about money.

The Financial Dependency Myth

Women have always been portrayed as financially dependent on men, whether in fairy tales or cultural Daisy Hill conventions. This myth upholds gender norms that restrict women's ability to manage their finances and the notion that they are incapable of doing so. But women are more than capable of taking control of their finances and establishing financial security on their terms.

The Need to Put Caregiving Before Career

Due to societal expectations, women are frequently under unwarranted pressure to put their jobs on the back burner in favor of caring for others, which can result in job gaps, lower earning potential, and less financial security. Giving care is vital, but it shouldn't come at the expense of a woman's financial security. Women can achieve both career success and financial independence by fighting for laws that promote work-life balance, questioning gender norms, and looking for equal partnerships.

The Shame Associated with Ambition and Money

Openly pursuing wealth and success exposes women to criticism and scrutiny; they are frequently called "greedy" or "ambitious." This stigma prevents women from negotiating for better pay, standing up for themselves on the job, or starting their businesses.

Daisy Hill

It's time to reject this unfair disparity and proudly accept our goals. Achieving financial success is a right that every woman should pursue, not a privilege exclusive to men.

The "Impulsive Shopper Myth"

The misconception that women are not responsible for money is perpetuated by their frequent portrayal as frivolous or impulsive consumers.

This myth ignores the structural obstacles that women must overcome to get financial resources and education, as well as the astute financial judgment that many of them exhibit daily. Women can be empowered to make confident and well-informed financial decisions if we challenge this misconception and support projects that promote financial literacy and address the needs of women.

The Quiet Regarding Money Issues

Lastly, the culture of guilt and quiet around money is one of the most pernicious financial stereotypes that affect women. Women are frequently dissuaded from discussing their money in public, which results in a lack of responsibility, openness, and support. By ending this

Daisy Hill

taboo and having candid discussions about money, women may give themselves and one another the confidence to take charge of their financial destiny.

Thought-Provoking Questions

✓ Which prevalent financial misconceptions have you personally encountered?

✓ What attitudes and actions have these misconceptions influenced about money?

✓ What aspects of gender and financial expectations have you internalized from society?

✓ What actions can you take in your own life to confront and dispel these assumptions?

✓ How can you encourage other women to pursue financial empowerment and challenge prevailing financial stereotypes?

Regaining our financial power as women requires us to recognize and confront financial stereotypes. We can start to break down the obstacles preventing us from achieving our goals and building a more equal and powerful financial future for ourselves and future generations by

Daisy Hill

acknowledging the gender biases and societal conventions that influence our views about money.

This chapter redefines spending as a tool for liberation rather than a source of constraint through relatable anecdotes, useful exercises, and guidance. Promoting deliberate, thoughtful spending that is in line with personal objectives and values, gives women the confidence to make decisions that support their financial well-being without fear of social rejection.

Come along on this life-changing journey toward a liberated spending philosophy that values individuality, empowers people, and welcomes financial freedom on our terms. It's time to reject social norms and build a future in which spending is an expression of individuality rather than compliance.

A Stacked Deck Against Women

Women have long been expected to be financially capable, but the sad truth is that no one has ever really taught them how. The system was not built for women or anyone who isn't a straight, cisgender white man.

So, when we as women are told to just be magically

Daisy Hill

good with money even though no one has ever taught us we are then scared to ask questions for fear of seeming dumb or naive.

It's a vicious cycle, but one that we can break if we're willing to educate ourselves and each other on financial matters. When we understand why shame is happening, that shame turns to anger at the unjust systems that cause it in the first place. Once we turn shame into anger, we can turn anger into powerful action.

The societal taboos around money are harmful and perpetuated by those in power to maintain control. This narrative leads us to feel shame about our financial situation and prevents us from being transparent about money. Talking about money is one of the biggest ways we can create systemic change.

Women feel shame and guilt around money, even when they are successful, due to social conditioning in childhood. Girls are not socialized to feel that it's okay for them to have ambition about creating wealth.

As a result, women are overrepresented in jobs such as nursing and teaching, or they perform unpaid domestic

Daisy Hill

labor important jobs that our economy devalues precisely because they are done mainly by women.

The world is built for boys and men to play in, while stores and malls are designed to tempt the impulse dollars of young women. Women are the most marketed to, but then they are shamed for spending money on things that bring them joy. It can be difficult for women to cut spending, as they constantly must spend money on clothing, food, and transportation. Meanwhile, men rarely must spend money on these things.

The emphasis on controlling spending is also unfair because it assumes that all women spend money on frivolous items. However, many women, especially black women, spend money on necessities but are still criticized for it. Spending money is not a bad thing. The classic question Are you a saver or a spender? is meant to make savers feel good and spenders feel ashamed, when in fact, that question is cr*p.

When it comes to spending money, most financial experts would tell you to cut back on it altogether. But for those who have learned how to use money as a tool to build a life they love; they'd tell you to spend money. You don't Daisy Hill have to stop spending money. You just must stop spending money on things you don't care about. This takes many forms, from impulsively clicking Add to Cart via an Instagram ad for $20 wrinkle-preventing stickers to going to an expensive museum on your vacation to Rome even though you're not a museum person.

Your Rich Life is the ideal life you want to be living. It's one where you look around at your finances, your relationships, and your ordinary Tuesday and say, wow, this is the kind of life I want to be living. You're going to write down everything you spend money on and how much it costs for one month. You're also going to write down why you made the purchase and how it made you feel.

To start your money diary, flip to the back pages of your handwritten day planner, open a fresh Google doc or sheet, or click the Notes app on your phone. There's no right method. Do what works for you. After a month, once the money diary is complete, you should review it.

We start by looking at our necessary expenses. These include rent, housing, groceries, transportation, health care, car insurance, and so on. We then want to look at Daisy Hill the want side of our needs. As we've discussed, the line between wants and needs is blurred.

I had lost my main client, and I didn't know how I was going to get income. I had one or maybe one and a half months' worth of emergency funds. I didn't know how much I needed to live.

When dealing with a customer service representative, be polite, and clear about your problem, and back your ask up with data. The Three Value Categories are the things in your life that bring you the most joy and provide you with the best return on happiness investment.

Your three value categories are spending money on things you love, less on things you don't love, and less on things you don't care about. You should spend your money on things you love and care about, and then save the rest.

Values-based spending is all about understanding what matters most to you and how you want to spend your money. It reflects your values, and it allows you to express those values through your spending.

It is important to be aware of your emotional state before making a purchase. If you are constantly buying things to
Daisy Hill

cope with life's difficulties, you are not fixing the fundamental issue of your unhealthy work environment.

By considering the purchase through the lens of what's important to you, you'll be able to determine if buying it is worth giving up something you value. For example, if you love traveling, you might consider your purchases in terms of where they'll get you in the world.

When it comes to buying items, consider their value to you. Is it worth the price you're paying? Is the quality of this item worth what you're paying for it? Will you get a lot of value from this item?

If you're spending money on something that you don't enjoy, it's a habit that isn't serving your wallet or your over-caffeinated body.

Ask yourself whether you enjoy and look forward to this thing or if you're just doing it because that's the way you've always done it.

Your hourly rate, which is the amount of money you make per hour, can be a good way to reflect on your output of work versus your spending. When you spend money on things you don't need or even want, it means
Daisy Hill

you're not able to save that money or spend it on something more valuable to you.

If we're going to use our financial education to fight patriarchy, we must make thoughtful spending decisions. We control more than 70 percent of consumer spending, and we can use that power to change the world.

The narrative around money that you hear in your circle may be different from what you hear from other sources. Do you feel pressured to save and stop spending frivolously?

After two weeks, review your purchases and answer the following questions: What went well during the last two weeks. What could be improved regarding your spending habits?

Name three worthwhile purchases. Name three things you bought that are no longer.

The patriarchy realizes that when a woman gains the knowledge to build wealth, soon it will have no control over her life or decisions. A woman's right to financial stability is a step toward making the world a better place.

Daisy Hill

CHAPTER THREE

Developing an Intentional Financial Mindset

We must develop a conscious money mindset in our pursuit of financial empowerment. Being attentive to our financial decisions, values, and habits entails being present, deliberate, and aware of them. We may harness the power of our thoughts and emotions to bring about positive change in our financial lives by practicing mindfulness and gaining a deeper knowledge of our connection with money. We will look at ways to develop a mindful money mentality and use it to control our finances in this chapter.

Six Easy Steps to Develop a Positive Money Mindset

- Please Pardon Your Previous Financial Errors. Nobody is flawless.

- Recognize Your Feelings and Thoughts About Money.

- Understand That It's a Losing Game to Compare Yourself to Others.

Daisy Hill

- Focus on Developing Positive Habits.

- Make a Budget That Makes You Happy.

- Never forget to express gratitude.

To cultivate a mindful money mindset, you must take a deliberate and conscious approach to managing your finances. It involves getting a deeper understanding of your thoughts, feelings, and behaviors related to money and using that understanding to make financially empowered decisions. The following is a summary of the steps involved in cultivating a mindful money mindset:

Awareness: Increasing your awareness of your financial habits, patterns, and beliefs is the first step towards developing a mindful money mindset.

This includes understanding your attitudes towards money, how you react to financial stressors, and you're spending and saving behaviors. By doing so, you can identify areas for improvement and make more deliberate financial decisions.

Purposeful financial objectives: Allocating your funds to the things that are most important to you requires

Daisy Hill

setting purposeful financial objectives. After taking the time to determine your priorities, values, and aspirations, make sure your goals are attainable and in line with them. Having clear goals for your finances provides you with direction and purpose, whether it's working off debt, saving for a certain purchase, or investing for the future.

Financial Self-Compassion: It's critical to treat yourself with kindness and compassion, particularly with money. Everyone experiences financial setbacks or mistakes from time to time, and punishing yourself for them will only make you feel more stressed. Rather, engage in self-compassionate practices by accepting your humanity, pardoning yourself for past transgressions, and drawing lessons from them to help you go forward with more courage and resilience.

Gratitude and Abundance: Two of the most important components of a mindful money mentality are practicing gratitude and acknowledging abundance. Practice being grateful for what you have rather than dwelling on your shortcomings or evaluating yourself against others. By adopting this new perspective, you can begin to see your blessings in terms of money and start thinking of it as

Daisy Hill

abundant rather than scarce.

Mindful Saving and Spending: Mindful saving and spending entail using your money with intention and deliberation. Think twice before you buy to make sure it fits with your priorities and values. Steer clear of impulsive purchases and place more value on long-term fulfillment than on momentary pleasure. In a similar vein, save money daily and watch what you consume to cut down on wasteful spending. In a similar vein, make sure you consistently save money and pay attention to your consumption patterns to save costs.

Bringing Mindfulness to Everyday Life: Developing a mindful financial mindset is a continuous process that goes beyond handling particular financial responsibilities. Look for methods to include mindfulness in your normal financial practices, such as keeping a record of your spending, periodically going over your budget, or expressing thanks for the gifts in your life.

By maintaining a state of awareness and mindfulness when making financial decisions, you can develop a more profound sense of empowerment, intentionality, and awareness.

Daisy Hill

In general, developing a mindful money mindset involves approaching your financial situation with awareness, attention, and compassion. You may design a better and more rewarding financial future for yourself by getting a better knowledge of your connection with money and applying mindfulness to inform your choices.

The Awareness's Power

A mindful money attitude begins with becoming conscious of our financial behaviors, routines, and beliefs. This is being aware of our attitudes and behaviors toward money, including how we spend, save, and invest. We can start to see places for improvement and change by being conscious of our money triggers, impulses, and motivations.

Reflection Questions

✓ How would you describe your current relationship with money? Is it mindful or reactive?

✓ What are some areas of your financial life where you could benefit from greater awareness and intentionality?

✓ What values and priorities are most important to

Daisy Hill

you when it comes to money?

✓ How can you practice gratitude and abundance in your financial life?

✓ What steps can you take to align your financial goals with your values and aspirations?

Cultivating a mindful money mindset is a transformative journey that empowers us to take control of our finances and create the life we desire. By developing awareness, practicing gratitude, setting intentional goals, and embracing self-compassion, we can harness the power of mindfulness to master our money and build a brighter, more abundant future

Daisy Hill

CHAPTER FOUR
Keys To Financial Game Plan

The Financial Game Plan is my checklist for working through your financial goals and figuring out your next steps. No matter if you're a budgeting queen, investment pro, or absolute finance newbie, this checklist will guide you through everything you need to have in place to make your financial goals achievable.

Your financial game plan should include a review of your assets and debts, a discussion of your financial goals, and action steps to get you moving in the right direction. This will help you create your plan for the next five to ten years. You should decide whether you would like to own a house or whether you would prefer to rent.

Creating a financial game plan involves several key steps to help you manage your money effectively and work towards your financial goals. Here is a structured approach:

Daisy Hill

Set Clear Goals: Define what you want to achieve financially. Whether it's buying a house, retiring comfortably, saving for education, or starting a business, having specific goals will guide your plan. Keep your expenses low. If your goal is to pay off your mortgage in four years, you may not be able to get a new car every two years.

Prioritize what is important and keep the rest of your expenses low. This does not mean that you cannot dine out three times a week, but maybe you can give up cable to keep your expenses low. I live in Florida and air conditioning is non-negotiable. For me, that means I might not dine at restaurants as often during the summer because my electric bill will be higher. Using the grill is a bonus!

Assess Your Current Situation: Take stock of your finances. Calculate your income, expenses, assets, and debts. Understanding where you stand will help you plan better.

Budgeting: Create a budget outlining your income and

Daisy Hill

expenses. Track your spending to ensure you are living within your means and allocating funds towards your goals.

Create A Savings Plan: The first step to managing your money is to be comfortable being uncomfortable. You want to change your relationship with money, and you need to create a plan to make it happen.

A good rule for them is to put 10% of each paycheck into a savings account. If you receive bonuses, overtime pay, or a tax refund, try and store the money aside without touching it. This will help you create an emergency fund for expenses such as car repair, home repair, or a medical emergency. Life will always have an unexpected event. Plan accordingly

Emergency Fund: Aim to build an emergency fund that covers 3-6 months of living expenses. This fund acts as a safety net during unexpected situations like job loss or medical emergencies.

Debt Management: If you have debts, prioritize paying them off. Focus on high-interest debts first while making minimum payments on others.

Daisy Hill

Investment Strategy: Determine your risk tolerance and investment goals. Explore various investment options like stocks, bonds, mutual funds, or real estate. Consider diversifying your portfolio for better risk management.

Include A Significant Other When The Time Is Right: Only you can know when to incorporate a significant other into your financial goals is the right time to incorporate a significant other into your financial goals.

A good rule of thumb is that a conversation about financial goals should take place before a wedding. It should also take place before you open a joint account or pay bills together. Good communication and a joint plan will certainly help a relationship.

Retirement Planning: Start saving for retirement early. Take advantage of retirement accounts like 401(k)s, IRAs, or pension plans. Maximize employer contributions and seek professional advice if needed.

Insurance Coverage: Evaluate your insurance needs. This includes health, life, disability, and property insurance. Ensure adequate coverage based on your Daisy Hill circumstances.

Create a spending plan: Make sure your spending plan includes all your expenses, whether they are monthly or not. Include your car insurance, pet supplies and veterinary care, and summer camp expenses.

Decide where you must spend your money and decide would like to spend your money. The sooner you can pay down your debt, the sooner you can start putting more money aside for your dreams and other financial goals.

Set yourself up for a major credit score. Excellent credit can help you with lower interest rates on mortgages and car loans. Major credit can help you open a new credit card in case of an emergency expense.

Review and Adjust: Regularly review your financial plan. Circumstances change, and so should your plan. Adjustments might be necessary due to life events, economic changes, or shifts in goals. Be open to changing up your plan. Life will change your direction more than once. Be open to the change. Review your financial game plan and decide what needs to change.
Daisy Hill

Do you need to decrease savings to address a new expense? Can you increase the amount you pay towards your mortgage every month because of a promotion? Do you need to cut expenses because of a hospitalization? Adapting your financial game plan to your current needs is important.

Seek Professional Advice: Consider consulting a financial advisor or planner, especially for complex financial matters. They can provide tailored advice based on your situation and goals.

Remember, a financial game plan is a dynamic document that evolves. Flexibility and adaptability are crucial. Start with small, achievable steps and gradually progress towards bigger financial milestones.

Financial Priority List

Creating a financial priority list is crucial for managing your money effectively and working towards your financial goals. Here is a general guide to help you prioritize your financial matters:

Emergency Fund: Establish an emergency fund to cover three to six months' worth of living expenses. This fund acts as a financial safety net in case of unexpected expenses or job loss.

High-Interest Debt: Prioritize paying off high-interest debts, such as credit card balances, to avoid accumulating excessive interest payments.

Budgeting: Develop a realistic budget to track your income and expenses. A budget is like the gas gauge in your car. You would not drive a car without knowing how much gas it had, so you do not want to spend money without knowing how much is in your account. You want to be able to enjoy the drive, knowing that you can easily get back home.

I created my budgeting system because none of the others worked for me. The 3 Bucket Budget is designed to take care of yourself financially first while allowing you to spend money guilt-free.

Everything you need to live is in bucket one. This includes bills, rent, insurance, groceries, loan payments, utility bills, and so on. You cannot cut off my left hand before you cancel my Spotify subscription, but since it is not essential to my life, it does not go in bucket one.

Daisy Hill

Money in Bucket #2 should be used to pay off your debt faster, and it can also go toward paying for financial self-care such as paying down debt and saving for the future.

Everything else goes into Bucket #3. This is the fun category, and it includes eating out, vacations, new clothes, Spotify subscriptions, plant rescuing, coffee, and anything else that is not necessary to your life but makes it worth living. To stay on track with your budget and goals, set visual reminders. I like to write on Post-it notes and vision boards. Categorize your spending to identify areas where you can cut back and save more.

Insurance: Ensure you have adequate insurance coverage, including health, life, and property insurance. Review and update your insurance policies as needed.

Education Savings: If you have children, consider saving for their education through accounts like a 529 plan. Start early to benefit from compounding interest.

Investing: Diversify your investment portfolio based on your risk tolerance and financial goals. There are two ways to set up automation: through your service provider or your bank.

Daisy Hill

With your service provider, you can usually authorize a voided check and an authorization form, or simply provide your bank account and routing numbers.

With your bank, you can direct portions of your paycheck to be directly deposited into different accounts. Regularly review and adjust your investments as needed.

Medium-Term Goals

Save for medium-term goals like buying a home, starting a business, or taking a major vacation. When setting your financial goals, be sure they are sticky, meaning not ridiculously unobtainable but also not easy. A good goal should feel a little intimidating. This way, if you hit your goal, you will feel even more accomplished.

To make your goals specific, turn the intention I want to save money into a goal. To make it timely, add I want to save $500 per month, or I will have three months of living expenses saved by the end of this year. Choose appropriate investment vehicles based on your timeline and risk tolerance.

Tax Planning: Be mindful of tax implications in your financial decisions. Explore tax-advantaged accounts and

Daisy Hill

strategies to minimize your tax burden.

Long-Term Goals

Identify and plan for long-term financial goals such as paying off your mortgage, financial independence, or leaving a legacy. The statement A goal without a plan is just a wish is important to write down and remind yourself of often.

It can be a scary realization that you are ultimately responsible for your money, but the realization that you can control only what you can control can be liberating. Continuously reassess and adjust your financial plan as circumstances change.

Lifestyle Choices: Evaluate and manage lifestyle choices that impact your finances, such as housing, transportation, and discretionary spending. It can be difficult for women to get their finances in order because we have been told for years that we're bad at math and that money isn't for women.

We need to understand that the responsibility of having our finances in order brings with it great freedom. Make

Daisy Hill

informed decisions to align your lifestyle with your financial goals.

Continuous Learning: Invest time in continuous financial education to stay informed about personal finance trends, strategies, and opportunities.

Remember that your financial priorities may evolve, and it is essential to revisit and adjust your financial plan regularly. Additionally, seeking professional financial advice can provide personalized guidance based on your unique circumstances and goals.

Daisy Hill

CHAPTER FIVE
Debt

Debt isn't always a bad thing. Avoiding debt at all costs is not realistic sometimes you need to borrow money to invest in something that will pay off later, like a business or an education Debt can be a significant financial burden, but there are steps you can take to manage it effectively:

Understand Your Debt: List out all your debts, including credit cards, loans, mortgages, and any other outstanding amounts. Note down interest rates, minimum payments, and due dates for each.

Create a Repayment Strategy: Consider using either the debt avalanche or debt snowball method.

Debt Avalanche: Focus on paying off debts with the highest interest rates first while making minimum payments on others.

Debt Snowball: Start by paying off the smallest debts first, regardless of interest rates, and then use the Daisy Hill momentum to tackle larger debts.

Budgeting and Cutting Expenses: Create a budget that prioritizes debt repayment. Cut unnecessary expenses and redirect that money towards paying off debts faster.

Increase Income: Look for opportunities to increase your income, such as taking on a side job, freelancing, or selling items you no longer need. Use this extra income to accelerate debt payments.

Negotiate with Creditors: Sometimes, creditors are willing to negotiate lower interest rates or payment plans to help you pay off the debt. Contact them and explain your situation; they might offer solutions.

Consolidate or Refinance: Consider consolidating multiple debts into a single loan or refinancing at a lower interest rate if possible. This can simplify payments and reduce overall interest costs.

Avoid Taking on New Debt: While repaying existing debts, try to avoid taking on new debt. Focus on changing spending habits and sticking to your budget.

Daisy Hill

Seek Financial Guidance: If you are struggling to manage your debt, seek advice from a credit counselor or financial advisor. They can offer personalized strategies and guidance.

Remember, managing debt takes time and discipline. Celebrate small victories along the way as you pay off each debt and stay committed to your repayment plan.

Daisy Hill

CHAPTER SIX
Investing

Investing should not be about trying to make a quick buck. It's a long game that necessitates perseverance and patience. The longer you retain your shares, the more likely you are to profit in the stock market. Long-term investing has shown to be a successful technique throughout history.

Investing Fear

The fear of investing in real estate is another common financial misconception among women. Many women are reluctant to invest in the stock market or other financial instruments, for a variety of reasons including ignorance, risk aversion, or feelings of inadequacy. However, we may overcome this anxiety and seize the opportunity it offers by being knowledgeable about investing and seeing its potential for accumulating wealth.

Investing can be a powerful tool for building wealth over time. Here are some key points to consider:

Set Clear Goals: Define your investment objectives.
Daisy Hill

Whether it is saving for retirement, buying a house, or generating passive income, having specific goals will guide your investment strategy.

Risk Tolerance: Understand your risk tolerance. Some investments carry higher risks but offer potentially higher returns, while others are more conservative. Your risk tolerance will influence your investment choices.

Diversification: Do not put all your eggs in one basket. Diversify your investments across different asset classes (stocks, bonds, real estate, etc.) to reduce risk. This way, if one investment performs poorly, others may balance it out.

Start Early and Be Consistent: Time in the market matters.

Starting early allows your investments to benefit from compound interest. Consistency in investing, even with lesser amounts, can lead to significant growth over time.

Educate Yourself: Learn about different investment options. Understand the basics of stocks, bonds, mutual funds, ETFs, real estate, and other investment vehicles. Consider reading books, attending seminars, or using Daisy Hill reputable financial resources.

Long-Term Approach: Investing is a long-term commitment. While short-term fluctuations are normal, a long-term perspective can help you ride out market volatility and benefit from overall market growth.

Regularly Review and Rebalance: Periodically review your investment portfolio. Rebalance it if needed to maintain your desired asset allocation based on changes in your goals, risk tolerance, or market conditions.

Consider Tax Implications: Understand the tax implications of your investments. Certain accounts like IRAs or 401(k)s offer tax advantages that can benefit your overall returns.

Seek Professional Advice: Consider consulting a financial advisor or planner, especially if you are new to investing or have complex financial goals. They can provide personalized advice based on your situation.

Stay Informed and Patient: Keep yourself informed about market trends and economic news but avoid making impulsive decisions based on short-term fluctuations. Patience is key in investing.
Daisy Hill

Remember, investing involves risks, and there are no guarantees of returns. However, a well-thought-out investment strategy aligned with your goals and risk tolerance can significantly increase your chances of achieving financial success over the long term.

Daisy Hill

CHAPTER SEVEN
Earning Money

Earning money is the foundation of financial stability. Here are some strategies to boost your earnings:

Develop Skills: Invest in developing skills that are in demand. This could be through formal education, online courses, workshops, or firsthand experience. Continuously improving your skills can make you more valuable in the job market or as an entrepreneur.

Explore Multiple Income Streams: Diversify your income sources. Consider part-time jobs, freelancing, consulting, or starting a side business. Multiple income streams can provide stability and increase your overall earning potential.

Negotiate and Advocate for Yourself: Do not shy away from negotiating your salary or rates. Research market rates for your skills and experience and confidently negotiate fair compensation. Also, seek opportunities for advancement within your current job.

Daisy Hill

Invest in Networking: Networking is crucial. Building professional relationships can open doors to new opportunities, collaborations, and potential clients. Attend industry events, join online communities, and maintain relationships with colleagues and mentors.

Monetize Hobbies and Passions: Explore ways to turn your hobbies or passions into income streams. Whether it is photography, writing, crafting, or any other skill you enjoy, there might be ways to monetize them through freelance work, selling products, or teaching.

Embrace Technology: Leverage technology to your advantage. Explore online platforms and tools that allow you to work remotely, start an online business, or offer services to a global audience.

Continuously Learn and Adapt: Industries and markets evolve. Stay updated with the latest trends, technologies, and developments in your field. Adaptability and a willingness to learn new things can keep you ahead in your career or business.

Financial Education and Investments: Invest in financial literacy and consider investing your earnings

Daisy Hill

wisely. Whether it is stocks, real estate, or other investment vehicles, making informed decisions about your money can help it grow over time.

Money is a Tool That We Use to Get Free

Money is a tool to be used in the fight against patriarchy. It is not the only answer to dismantling patriarchy. When we talk about being financial feminists, we need to discuss the discrimination that keeps women out of C Suite positions.

We need to address the pay gap between white women and Latinas. It must be acknowledged that there is a hierarchy even within the word 'women' and that until all of us are free, no one is truly free.

Financial feminism is the child of the feminist and womanist movements that have come before it. It wouldn't be possible without the work that previous generations have done to get women into the workplace, to break down the barriers to women controlling their capital. It is the natural extension of the fight for equality.

The work of financial feminism must extend beyond individuals because the work of feminism does.

Daisy Hill

To focus the conversation on simply growing wealth is to stop short of the finish line. It leaves your sisters out in the cold, instead of inviting them inside beside the fire.

Remember, building a sustainable income takes time and effort. Stay focused, be adaptable, and be open to exploring new opportunities that align with your skills and interests.

Daisy Hill

CHAPTER EIGHT
Living A Financial Feminist Lifestyle

Living a financial feminist lifestyle involves embracing financial independence, equality, and empowerment for all genders. Here are some principles that align with this approach:

Equal Pay and Opportunity: Advocate for equal pay and opportunities in the workplace. Know your worth, negotiate for fair compensation, and support policies and organizations that promote gender equality in pay and career advancement.

Financial Literacy: Educate yourself and others about personal finance. Understand financial concepts, investing, budgeting, and saving. Encourage financial education for everyone, regardless of gender.

Financial Independence: Strive for financial independence regardless of gender. Aim to manage your finances autonomously, make informed financial

Daisy Hill

decisions, and have control over your money.

Supporting Women-Owned Businesses: Consider supporting businesses owned or led by women. This can be through purchasing products or services, investing in women-led ventures, or mentoring aspiring female entrepreneurs.

Breaking Stereotypes: Challenge gender stereotypes surrounding money. Encourage discussions about finances and empower women to take charge of their financial future.

Investing in Education and Skills: Support education and skill development for all genders. Encourage girls and young women to pursue STEM fields and other traditionally male-dominated professions to increase earning potential.

Advocacy and Activism: Get involved in advocating for policies that promote gender equality in finance, such as parental leave, flexible work hours, and equal access to financial services.

Financial Safety and Security: Take steps to ensure financial safety and security, including having emergency
Daisy Hill

funds, adequate insurance coverage, and understanding legal and financial rights.

Living a financial feminist lifestyle is about fostering equality, empowerment, and financial autonomy for all individuals. It involves challenging societal norms, promoting education and opportunity, and advocating for fair treatment and representation in financial matters.

Why Should You Care About Financial Feminism?

Well-managed finances are often the key to success in any adult's life. Navigating the financial sphere, like paying off bills, saving for retirement, paying taxes, and managing your day-to-day expenses, is already difficult enough as it is. Dealing with gender-specific financial struggles on top of that can make it even more confusing, frustrating, and unbearable.

Financial feminism is all about addressing just that and more by empowering women to make their own financial decisions. Women are paid less than men, we already know that. But they also may lack the financial literacy skills and confidence to invest and save money, level up in their careers, and manage their finances.

Daisy Hill

Financial literacy starts at a young age, and several studies have proven that inequality starts young: boys receive more allowance than girls growing up often for less work. That disparity continues into adulthood.

According to the Global Gender Gap Report 2021, women still earn only eighty-six cents to a man's dollar for a similar role. In fact, in the U.S., women earn less than men in all occupations. And the pandemic has set back women's labor force participation for more than 30 years, which will undoubtedly have a significant impact on women's collective financial freedom.

Furthermore, women tend to live longer lives than men. Researchers in Germany estimate that 75% of women aged 35 to 50 are at risk of poverty in old age because they are not adequately preparing and saving for retirement.

The long and the short of it? Women earn proportionately less than their male counterparts, and lower labor market participation and other systemic biases compound that effect. As a result, women are far less likely to invest and build wealth throughout their lives.
Daisy Hill

Why Is Financial Independence Important For Women?

Financial feminism is a lifestyle of learning and growing, and it takes vulnerability, consistency, and grace. But this movement is bigger than just us as individuals. When we commit to bettering our own financial lives, we start changing the equation.

When you manage your income and plan for your financial future, you have far more power to decide on your own choices in life. Do you want to have a baby? Do you want to travel the world for five years? Do you want to focus on your career? Do you want ALL these things? These life choices can change the course of your life, and finances give you the power to make those decisions for yourself. You do not have to be dependent on someone else's money if you do not want to even if you're married.

It is especially important because the financial inequality between men and women continues throughout their whole lives. And, throughout their lives, women often end up with less retirement savings than men despite living far longer.

Daisy Hill

According to a 2016 study by the National Institute on Retirement Security (NIRS), the median household income of women sixty-five and older was $47,244; however, for men, it was $57,144. In other words, retired women had 83% of the median household income as men the same age.

How Can You Take Control Of Your Financial Future?

Financial feminism helps tackle systemic institutions by engaging, educating, and encouraging more women to take back control of their finances. Here is how you can join the movement:

Be fearless: It is okay not to have all the answers. Women consistently lag men in financial literacy, and it impacts their ability to make better financial decisions. That means women feel more intimidated by investing, retirement planning, and wealth building.

Research shows that one-third of the gender financial literacy gap can be explained by women's lack of confidence. "When it comes to financial literacy, women know less than men, but they know more than they think they know," the paper concludes.

Daisy Hill

It is all about being fearless, and that comes down to confidence. So how do you build confidence in the financial world? Try these tips:

- ✓ Invest insignificant amounts of money in the stock market, so you learn by doing.

- ✓ Educate the younger generation about financial topics early. This is so important if you have children!

- ✓ Ask your friends and family what they might be doing.

- ✓ Ask for professional help.

Daisy Hill

Chapter NINE
Rewrite your Financial Story

In a society where women have historically been underrepresented in financial affairs, now is the moment to take back control of your story and usher in a new era of financial freedom and empowerment, rewrite your financial story to fit your values, ambitions, and goals.

Examining Your History

Thinking back on your prior financial experiences is the first step in writing a new chapter in your financial tale. Examine the ideas, dispositions, and actions that have influenced your current financial relationship. Were you brought up to think that money was plentiful or in short supply? Did you see your family have financial hardships or successes? You may start to rewrite your financial story in a way that gives you the confidence to take charge of your future by knowing where it came from.

Recognizing Limiting Thoughts

Daisy Hill

Finding any limiting thoughts that might be preventing you from achieving financial success is crucial. These convictions could include ideas like "I'll never be wealthy" or "I'm not good with money." You can replace these constricting ideas with empowering ones that support your ability to achieve financial stability and prosperity by identifying and disputing these constricting ones.

Creating New Budgetary Objectives

After recognizing and reframing your limiting beliefs, it's important to make new financial goals that align with your aspirations and values. Whether you want to start a business, pay off debt, save for emergencies, or retire early, make sure your goals are clear, quantifiable, and doable. You may steer clear of financial failure and toward fulfillment by establishing specific objectives and a plan for reaching them.

Formulating a Budget

Making a financial plan with your objectives in mind is crucial because it will show you how to get there.

Daisy Hill

Tailoring tactics for budgeting, saving, investing, and debt management to your specific financial circumstances and priorities should be part of this approach. By managing proactively, you take charge of your finances, you may establish a strong base for sustained financial success.

Daisy Hill

Adopting a Resilient Finance

Throughout the process of rewriting your financial story, difficulties and disappointments will unavoidably arise. But in the face of difficulty, it's critical to develop resilience and tenacity. Recall that obstacles are chances for development and education rather than signs of failure. You can conquer any obstacles in your path and come out stronger and more confident than before if you embrace resilience and remain dedicated to your financial objectives.

Honoring Your Achievements

Lastly, remember to recognize and honor your accomplishments along the route. Whether it's accomplishing a debt repayment milestone, a savings milestone, or a financial objective, take the time to recognize and honor your accomplishments. Honoring your accomplishments strengthens your resolve to change your financial narrative and build the life you want, in addition to giving you more self-assurance and determination.

Daisy Hill

Talk About Money

As I have mentioned previously, many people are taught from an early age to avoid conversations about money, and that's especially true for women. That means how much you make, how much your coworkers make, how much you budget… The list goes on.

According to the Ellevest Financial Wellness Survey 2021, only 14% of women said they regularly talk with others when looking for support and guidance. In the same survey, half of women (45%) reported that talking about money helps them feel more supported, reduces stress (41%), and makes them feel more informed about their own financial decisions (39%). It can be difficult to talk about money, especially when there's so much shame and secrecy surrounding the topic. It is not normalized. That is why it is so important to keep speaking up and talking about money.

When you start talking about money with your friends, coworkers, family, and partner, you understand what is possible and what is not possible. (Did you know that couples that openly discuss their finances report being far
Daisy Hill

happier?)

You may learn you are being underpaid, or that you can uniquely reimagine your budget.

Or you are reminded to start focusing on saving more. It does not have to be awkward, and the more we normalize having conversations around money, the less uncomfortable it will be.

Surround Yourself With Positive Influences

You may not feel comfortable speaking with friends or family yet. That is okay. One thing you can do right now is start surrounding yourself with positive financial role models and financial educators, both online and offline. For example, social media influencer Tori Dunlap, the woman behind Her First 100K, offers online advice to women specifically to help them learn more about setting themselves up for success. Another financial educator online: Bola Sokunbi of Clever Girl Finance.

Surrounding yourself with these voices will help normalize talking about money, investing, and building wealth.

Daisy Hill

Speak Up At Work

For so many people, the discussions about money begin at work. The more you can improve the situation in your own office, the better you make it for all your fellow women. If you feel like you can speak up at work, consider advocating for things that will help women in your office, like paid family leave, more vacation time, flexible working policies, and more.

It also means speaking up for yourself. Advocating to be paid the same as your male counterparts can be difficult to navigate. You may even feel like you have a case of imposter syndrome. But the truth is, negotiating at work can make a substantial difference.

If you feel like you could improve your negotiation skills, I highly recommend AAUW's free online salary negotiation course. You can access the course here.

Have Your Accounts

Whether you are married or living with your expenses mixed, consider having your financial accounts. You can still contribute to the household expenses while managing your own money. Having your account not only helps

Daisy Hill

with feelings of self-worth, but it can also help you in case an emergency arises.

Even if you have a strong relationship, it is important to keep at least one account of your own.

Have Individual Goals

Women should always have their own financial goals, no matter their relationship status. Your individual goals and your goals with your partner can help you get ahead in life, whether that means paying off your student loans early or setting aside money for your child's future.

Conclusion

"Financial Feminist Master: Your Money and Create the Life You Love" concludes with certain chapters. Despite the Patriarchy's Cr*p "We set out on a life-changing adventure that breaks through conventional limits and gives each reader the ability to take control of their own financial story. This book dissolves the structural obstacles embedded in the patriarchal frameworks that have long restricted our financial freedom, acting as a beacon of guidance as we traverse the treacherous terrain of personal finance.

A new financial paradigm one that is inclusive, empowering, and fundamentally feminist emerges in the book's last pages. It invites readers to reject social conventions and embrace financial freedom as a necessary step toward self-actualization. By promoting a thorough grasp of financial literacy, and eliminating financial stereotypes based on gender, this book gives its readers the knowledge to successfully navigate the financial world while simultaneously instilling a revolutionary attitude using useful instruments for wealth Daisy Hill development.

Every financial feminist is urged to take her route toward economic emancipation as the journey ends with a call to action.

Readers are equipped to negotiate the financial world with confidence, resilience, and an unrelenting commitment to building the life they love, thanks to their newly acquired wisdom and tenacious spirit. This is more than simply a financial manual; it is a call to action, an endorsement of the strength of financial feminism, and a proclamation that everyone can rewrite their own financial story.

In the book's concluding remarks, "Financial Feminist Master," the author pushes readers to continue the financial empowerment movement and to question and destroy patriarchal standards. As the book ends, it leaves an impression on the readers' hearts and minds, motivating them to create a future in which personal fulfillment and financial equality coexist, escaping the constraints of patriarchy, and paving the way for a life of plenty, independence, and unabashed joy.

Daisy Hill

Other Books

Money Management "Managing Money At All   Ages"

https://kdp.amazon.com/action/dualbookshelf.kindl epromotions/en_US/marketing/A31RXBY5JZ7QCV/p romotio n-manager?ref_=kdp_BS_D_ta_pa_main

How Motivation Can Improve Your Work Productivity "Unleashing the Motivation Power: A Guide to Boosting Workplace Productivity"

https://kdp.amazon.com/action/dualbookshelf.kindl epro motions/en_US/marketing/A1OMVY2XGR2VP1/pro motion-manager?ref_=kdp_BS_D_ta_pa_main

Music Therapy for Pain Relief: Healing through Harmony for all Ages

https://www.amazon.com/MUSIC-THERAPY-PAIN-RELIEF-HEALING-ebook/dp/B0CN3BG8LK?ref_=ast_author_dp

FIT TIME MANAGEMENT "Making Workouts a Priority in a Busy Schedule https://a.co/d/2r12LBs

Daisy Hill

www.ingramcontent.com/pod-product-compliance
Lightning Source LLC
Chambersburg PA
CBHW071059290526
45795CB00004B/1567